Lost In Michigan's
Ghost Towns
and Similar Places

⬧ETAOIN PUBLISHING⬧
www.etaoinpublishing.com

HURON
PHOTO.COM

Publisher: Etaoin Publishing and Huron Photo LLC
             Saginaw, MI
             www.EtaoinPublishing.com
             www.HuronPhoto.com

Ordering Information:
Books may be ordered from www.LostinMichigan.net

Printed in the United States of America

ISBN 978-1-955474-20-7

Dedicated to the poeple that lived, worked, and died in Michgan's small towns. May thier towns history not be forgotten

Introduction

Michigan has several ghost towns scattered throughout the Upper and Lower Peninsulas. Many were old lumbering towns, and when the sawmill moved, because the timber was all cut down, the town moved with it. Some towns just faded away as larger cities dominated the region or grew in size and villages were annexed into it. Whatever the reason, they disappeared, but their name still shows up on a map. In some of the Great Lakes State ghost towns, only a few things remain or it is completely gone. I have listed some of my favorite ghost towns and forgotten villages that I have visited in my travels over the years. I have also listed some places that were not actual towns but are like ghost towns and worth visiting if you enjoy traveling around Michigan.

Michigan ghost towns are not like the ones in the American southwest. The hot dry air preserves wood, and buildings can stand for a long time in the desert sand.

Michigan's spring rains and heavy snow in the winter can destroy an abandoned building rapidly. There still are some ghost towns in Michigan where old structures still stand either by luck or preservation.

Some of the towns are historic sites open to the public, while some are still occupied by a few residents. If you visit any of these places, please be respectful of any no trespassing signs and follow any posted rules. Hopefully, these places will be around for generations to learn about Michigan's Past.

Contents

Chapter One
Southern Lower Peninsula

Chapter 2
Central Lower Peninsula

Chapter 3
Northern Lower Peninsula

Chapter 4
Upper Peninsula

Chapter One
Southern Lower Peninsula

The Hidden Town of Singapore

Singapore circa 1850

Location:
Under the dunes north of the Kalamazoo River near the mouth. It is private property and not accessible to the public.

A historical marker for the town is located in front of city hall in Saugatuck
102 Butler St,
Saugatuck, MI 49453
42.65497, -86.20427

When most people think of ghost towns they think of abandoned wooden buildings sitting on the sand of the American southwest. The town of Singapore in Michigan's southwest is buried under the sand.

Singapore early 1900s

Singapore sat near the mouth of the Kalamazoo River on the Lake Michigan shoreline. It was founded in the 1830s by New York land speculators who hoped it would grow into a large city. By the 1870s, it was a prosperous lumber town with three mills, two hotels, several general stores, and a renowned "Wild-cat" bank. After the trees were all cut, the mills closed and many of the residents moved on to other cities. Many of the houses and buildings were moved or torn down, but a few remained. Over time, the wind from Lake Michigan shifted the sand and covered up the townsite of Singapore. It was located somewhere along Saugatuck Beach Road, and some people say sometimes the wind will shift the sand around and reveal the tops of a building for a short period of time. A historical marker stands next to the Saugatuck City Hall reminding people of the town hidden beneath the sand.

A wild cat bank was one that printed its own currency but whose notes were backed by overvalued securities. In 1837, Michigan passed the General Banking Act, which allowed any group of landowners to organize a bank by raising at least $50,000.

The Good Old Days in Jones

Location:
Main Street
Jones, MI 49061
41.902343, -85.798903

West of the town of Three Rivers is a small town by the name of Jones. In 1831, the area was settled by John Blair and Daniel Driskel. The nearby lake was named Driskel Lake. The first businesses in the town were owned by William D. Jones, and after platting the village, he named

5

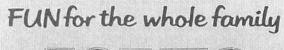

There are loads of things to see, do and enjoy. Truly unique shops, lots of animals and exhibits. Places of fun and education. Memory Lane has something for everyone in the family to enjoy just the way it was in the "good ol' days."

Newspaper advertizement for Jones

it after himself. William's son, E.H. Jones, became the first postmaster in 1881.

For decades Jones was an average little Michigan town where people lived, worked and went about their daily business without any fanfare. In the 1970s, a man by the name of Edward Lowe decided to convert the small downtown district to look like a wild west town like something from an old western movie set. You probably think it was a strange and crazy idea, but unlike other people, Mr. Lowe had a vast fortune to implement his plans. How Ed Lowe acquired his wealth is an American entrepreneurial tale that most people don't know even though the product he invented is still used by millions every day.

In the 1940s, cats did their business in a litter box filled with sand or dirt. One day, Ed Lowe's neighbor asked him for some sand for her litter box. He worked at his family's ice and coal company and had some dried clay that was used to soak up spills. He gave her some of these dried up clay granules to try instead, thinking they would work better than sand. She was amazed at how well it worked, and Ed's multi-million dollar business, Kitty Litter and Tidy Cat, was born.

Mr. Lowe updated the little town of Jones with some of the profits from his Kitty Litter sales. I think he was sure tourism would flourish since Swiss Valley Ski Resort was only a few miles away. Sadly, the town did not attract the business Lowe was hoping for, and the buildings slowly faded away. The town of Jones has several residents and is not a true "ghost town", but the buildings along Main Street still have some remnants of the former tourist attraction facades. It's like a ghost town of a fake ghost town.

Mary's City of David

Location:
1158 E Britain Ave,
Benton Harbor, MI 49022
42.1087204, -86.43039

Near Benton Harbor is a massive palatial-looking building. It was part of the Israelite House Of David. A few hundred yards down the street is Mary's City Of David. It was not a city nor is it a ghost town per se, but it was a little community that has been somewhat deserted.

The House of David is a religious commune that was founded by Benjamin and Mary Purnell in 1903. Benjamin Purnell was a traveling preacher from Kentucky who one day declared himself the seventh and final messenger of God, as foretold in the Book of Revelation. He promised eternal life to all those who joined his commune. He believed they should be more like Jesus, and not cut their hair, including the men. The male members of the commune stood out in Benton Harbor with their long hair flowing down to their waist. They were prohibited from using alcohol, tobacco, eating meat, owning property, and were to remain celibate.

Despite these downsides, the House of David grew to hundreds of members by 1906, and they owned thousands of acres. They planted orchards and grew crops in their fields. They harvested enough fruit that they had their own cannery and operated a power plant to supply electricity. They were a self-sufficient group that had their own carpentry shop, tailor shop and laundry.

The group became rather wealthy and well liked by the public until the 1920s, when thirteen young women confessed to having intercourse with the group's leader Benjamin Purnell when they were minors. After a lengthy and public trial, he was not convicted of having relations with minors, but he was convicted of fraud. Purnell died in 1927 before he was sentenced. The accusations caused the commune to split with Benjamin's wife Mary Purnell taking half its members and creating a new commune down the street known as Mary's City of David.

Over time, membership in the commune declined; today Mary's City of David has several little houses in rows along the streets. Some of the main buildings are still standing but are in need of repair. In 2009, it was designated a historic district and placed on the National Register of Historic Places. The auditorium has been converted into a museum and the bakery a gift shop. If you go exploring around the area, know that it is privately owned so please be respectful.

Eden Springs Park, located nearby, was an amusement park created by the House of David. It has reopened, and the owners have restored one of the trains. The park is not what it used to be, but the train still gives rides to passengers.

The Underwater Town of Rawsonville

Rawsonville circa 1890

Location:
Under Belleville Lake

Van Buren Park
50901 S Interstate 94 Service Dr,
Van Buren Charter Township,
MI 48111
42.218181, -83.5382452

The current town of Rawsonville is located next to I-94 south of Willow Run Airport near Ypsilanti. The original town of Rawsonville is under water. It was originally platted by Amariah Rawson next to the Huron River in the 1830s. The town began to grow after a grist mill was built on the river and attracted many residents. By the time of the Civil War, the community was thriving, and it even had a wagon and stove manufacturing business.

After the war the railroad bypassed the town, it was not long when Rawsonville's businesses began to struggle and people moved away. Some of the people stayed, and a few houses and buildings remained. In 1925, the Detroit Edison company constructed the French Landing hydroelectric dam on the Huron River and created Bellville Lake. The old village of Rawsonville became completely submerged; a historical marker stands in front of McDonalds as a reminder of the sunken city. Unfortunately, there is nothing to see of the former town of Rawsonville, but Bellview Lake has some beautiful parks to enjoy and fish to be caught.

Fallasburg and the Bridge

Location:
13893 Covered Bridge Rd NE,
Lowell, MI 49331
42.9813368, -85.3248503

Michigan has only a few covered bridges that you can drive your vehicle across. One of those bridges is the historic Fallasburg Bridge a few miles north of Lowell near Grand Rapids. On the north side of the bridge is the old historic town of Fallasburg. The schoolhouse, post office and houses make up the historic district of Fallasburg Pioneer Village.

John and Silas Fallas came to the area from New York in 1837 and built a sawmill and chair factory. The Flat River and hardwood forests that lined it made an excellent location for lumbering. The brothers built a grist mill for grinding grains, which was powered by a water wheel turned by the current of the river. The biggest challenge they faced was crossing the river. In 1840, the brothers built the first bridge to cross the river. This bridge was destroyed by the ice flows and rising water in the spring. The next two bridges survived a little while longer, and the town began to prosper.

With the sawmill, grist mill and bridge, the town thrived. The main road from Grand Rapids to Detroit came through the town that had been named after the brothers. The town of Fallasburg began to decline after the railroad decided the train would pass through the nearby town of Lowell, bypassing the once bustling little community. The covered bridge was built in 1871 in hopes that it would make traveling to the town easier, but the iron horse was far superior to the real ones that pulled wagons. After the dam was built in Lowell, the river no longer flowed like it used to, and the once mighty river no longer had the power to run the mill. The town basically disappeared from the map after that.

The town is now a historic village. The schoolhouse is open most Sundays in the summer months, and tours of some of the homes are given at different times. It is a nice drive across the bridge and through the historic village. The park makes a great place for a picnic.

Charlton Park

Location:
2545 S Charlton Park Rd.
Hastings, MI 49058
42.6189681, -85.2062204

Southeast of Hastings, along the Thornapple River, is a small village that seems to be stuck in time: a church, blacksmith shop, barber shop, general store, and several other buildings that look like they belong in the late 1800s.

17

Although they were built in the 1800s, they did not originally stand where they do today.

In 1936, Irving Charlton donated property to Barry County for a park. Over the years, several historic buildings from around Barry County were moved to the park. Today they create a historic village which includes the two-story brick building that served as the offices for the Hastings Mutual Insurance Co from 1908 to 1924. Visitors can explore the historic buildings along with a museum that displays artifacts collected by Irving Charlton. During the summer months, the park hosts several events such as car shows, tractor shows and Civil War reenactments. It was never an official town, but walking through the collection of historic buildings is similar to one, especially if you visit on a day when the buildings are closed and you are the only one there. You can learn more at their website www.Charltonpark.org.

Waterville

Location:
7034 MacArthur Rd
Saranac, MI 48881
42.91148439, -85.2139529

Not far from the town of Saranac is an old mill with a sign on it that reads Waterville Mill. It is all that remains of the old town of Waterville. In 1836, Robert Hilton from Grand Rapids purchased the large tract of land and platted a village he named Waterville. Hilton believed the

19

town would prosper from people visiting it as they traveled along the planned Grand River Turnpike.

To help the little town prosper, he gave land to James Hoag to build a mill. In 1838, Hoag opened his mill and store, and it became the post office for Waterville. Unfortunately, the turnpike never came through the little town. About a year after the post office opened, it was moved to Saranac. The old mill with its whimsically painted boards covering the windows still stands as a reminder of the short-lived town of Waterville. Hoag continued living in Waterville and ran his mill until he died when a tree fell on him in 1851. The old mill is near the road but privately owned, so please be respectful of the owners and do not trespass.

> If you are in the area, Sarnac has a wonderful old train station along the Fred Meijer Grand River Valley Trail that is now a museum.

Chapter Two
Central Lower Peninsula

Melbourne And The Boxing Champion

Location:
The exact location of the town is not known, but it was next to the Saginaw River on Melbourne Road North of Zilwaukee.

Approximately
43.5035640, -83.8942978

The Zilwaukee Bridge carries I-75 traffic over the Saginaw River. About a mile north of the bridge on the west side of the river is where the town of Melbourne was. It was founded by Wellington R. Burt in 1867 with a station located on the Saginaw and Mackinac Railroad line that ran between Saginaw and Bay City. Burt had recently visited Australia and liked the city of Melbourne, so he named the town after the city.

The Sawmill in Melbourne was said to be the largest sawmill in the world at the time. I am not sure if that is true, but there were several saw mills in the town besides Burt's, along with a shingle mill, a barrel works, and a salt processing plant. There were about 50 houses and some barracks for the unmarried workers, and a library and a school for the workers' children. In 1877, the town suffered from a devastating fire, but it did not completely wipe the town off the face of the earth, like some reports I have found stated, I think at that point, Wellington Burt did not want to rebuild his sawmill. After the fire, David Whitney Jr. of Detroit and Henry Batchelor of Bay City built a sawmill in Melbourne, along with a salt works and barrel plant. The sawmill produced over 30,000,000 feet of lumber a year.

A famous resident of Melbourne was George "Kid" Lavigne, whose parents moved from Bay City to Melbourne in 1880 where his father worked at Whitney and Batchelor, and in his youth, George worked as a cooper making barrels to ship salt. Lavigne, also known as "The Saginaw Kid" was boxing's first widely recognized World Lightweight champion when he won the title in 1896.

Melbourne was destroyed by another fire in 1894, and they made the decision not to rebuild the mill. By then the lumber industry was slowing down with much of the white pine trees in the Saginaw Valley were gone. The company sold the remaining houses for a few dollars to anyone who wanted to move them a few miles to Zilwaukee. In the early 1900s, an amusement park named Melbourne Park was built, but it went out of business a few years later. Strangely, it was used as a nudist colony for a short time, but apparently the cold Michigan weather was not a suitable climate for such a thing. Nothing remains of the town of Melbourne today; but who knows, maybe someone in Zilwaukee is living in George "Kid" Lavigne's old house.

Forester's Tragic Tale

Old Schoolhouse in Forester

Location:
Lake Huron Shoreline
M-25 a few miles north of M-46

Forester Cemetery
2631 N Lakeshore Rd,
Carsonville, MI 48419
43.5035653, -82.569396

It's hard to imagine that Michigan's Thumb was once covered in a thick dense forest. It is mostly farmland today because the lumberjacks harvested most of the timber. The town of Forester sits along the Lake Huron Shoreline a few miles north of Port Sanilac. It is not a ghost town, but there are only a few houses and businesses remaining from its lumbering heyday when ships tied up to the docks to fill their cargo holds and decks full of lumber. An old schoolhouse is hidden in the trees behind the township hall. It is there that the town's most famous resident most likely attended classes.

Fifteen-year-old Minnie Quay met a young man who worked on one of the cargo ships and fell madly in love with him. Minnie's family owned a tavern in Forester and her mother did not approve of Minnie's relationship with a sailor. Townspeople have said that her mother told Minnie she would rather see her dead than marry a sailor. Her mother would not allow Minnie to see the man she loved, and she never said goodbye to him the last time his ship sailed away from Forester.

A few days later word came back to Forester that the ship had sunk in a storm on the Great Lakes and all the crewmen drowned. Minnie was devastated upon hearing the news of her lover's death. About a week

Forester Circa 1910

later on April 27, 1876, her parents had to go on a trip and left Minnie at home to watch her infant brother. While her brother lay sleeping, she put on her white dress and walked out of her house. Passing the Tanner Inn, she waved to the people on the porch who said hello. She continued walking to the end of the dock that stretched out into Lake Huron. The people at the Tanner Inn watched in horror when she jumped into the frigid water without hesitation. An hour later, her lifeless body was pulled from the freezing cold water by men with grappling hooks.

She was laid to rest in the Forester Township Cemetery along Lake Huron north of town. Many people say that they have seen a young woman in white roaming the beaches. It's believed to be Minnie's spirit waiting for her sailor to return. People like to visit Minnie's grave and leave a coin or trinket on her tombstone. If you go to the cemetery to pay your respects to Minnie, be sure to drive through town and wonder what it must have been like back in the lumbering days.

The building that the Tanner Inn occupied is still standing in Forester today. During Prohibition, it was used as a speakeasy.

Wahjamega

Location:
M-81 and South Graf Road across from the airport west of Caro
43.4517247, -83.44532

If you are traveling in the Thumb on M-81 west of Caro, you may see a strange complex of buildings. They look out of place in Michigan with the tan stucco exterior and dark reddish brown tile roofs. When I saw them for the first time, they looked like they were part of an elaborate resort, but the truth is far more interesting. I always thought it was a Native American

31

name, but the name Wahjamega is an acronym from the initials of three partners who operated a sawmill here: William A Heartt, James A. Montgomery, and Edgar George Avery. They started the mill in 1852, and by 1853, the town was large enough that it was granted a post office. William A. Heartt was the first postmaster. By 1905, the lumber boom was over. The town's population declined, and the post office was closed.

In 1914, The Farm Colony for Epileptics was established in Wahjamega by the state and was devoted to the treatment of epilepsy. Much of the original population of the facility was moved from the overcrowded Lapeer State Home for Epileptics. The site was chosen for its rich soil and access to the railroad. The colony grew to include six houses, a hotel building, a store, barns and a blacksmith shop. There were several other small buildings such as a milk house, an ice house, and a chicken house. The farm also included a 40-acre apple tree orchard.

By 1925, the colony had a population of 800 people. In 1937, the name was changed to the Caro State Hospital for Epileptics and farming operations ceased in 1950. The population of the hospital continued to grow, and at its peak in 1967, there were 1800 people living and working at the facility.

The population began its decline as the state of Michigan changed its laws and how it cared for mentally ill residents. Over time the buildings became dilapidated and many are no longer used. The main building houses the Caro Center, a mental health facility run by the state, and is Tuscola County's second largest employer. The state has begun razing some of the old buildings that have been abandoned years ago. Besides the Caro Center, some houses and a stone church remain. I am not sure if the church goes back to the original town started by the lumbermen, but it is a beautiful little church.

In 1923, Michigan passed a eugenics law requiring the sterilization of feeble-minded and insane people. Over 3700 people in Michigan institutions were sterilized by surgery or x-rays. Both men and women were forced to have the procedure as recently as 1963.

The Concrete Town of Marlborough

Location:
8543 James Rd,
Baldwin, MI 49304
43.860276, -85.8411762
Private Property but you can view
a building from the road.

A few miles southeast of Baldwin, in the center of the Lower Peninsula, is a massive concrete building. The concrete is crumbling because it is one of the oldest concrete buildings in the state. The Great Northern Portland Cement Company constructed it as part of a cement plant in the 1890s to produce cement from a type of clay called marl that it harvested at a nearby lake. The town of Marlborough, named for the raw material, was created for the workers.

Production boomed, and by 1905, Marlborough had four hundred citizens. Marlborough once contained over seventy houses, an opera house, school and post office, and an 88-room hotel. After the plant was constructed, the cement it produced was inferior to other competitors. Production was costly, and the enormous energy demands of the plant required the construction of a massive power plant. It was the largest power plant in the Lower Peninsula at the time.

In the early 1900s, limestone was found on the Lake Huron shoreline near Alpena. The cost to produce cement with this limestone was much cheaper than in Marlborough. The Great Northern Portland Cement Company entered receivership in 1906, and the village houses were sold for salvage. The plant was dynamited for scrap iron, and by 1910, only the ruins of the plant remained.

The enormous concrete building still stands near the road. In the nearby forest is a labyrinth of concrete walls that are slowly being consumed by nature. It was designated as a Michigan State Historic Site in 1971. The property is closed to the public, but you can see one of the old buildings from the road.

Ora Labora

Location:
The Old Bay Port Cemetery
At the end of Sand Rd. off M-25
northeast of Bay Port
43.8588633, -83.3456161

At the end of Sand Road northeast of Bayport is the Old Bayport Cemetery. It sits on a hill with large trees standing between the tombstones and monuments. I imagine when the cemetery was created over 150 years ago, the trees were just little saplings. The old cemetery is the final resting place for some of the people of the Ora Labora colony.

The colony was formed in 1862 when Rev. Emil Baur purchased 740 acres on Wild Fowl Bay. He borrowed $20,000 from the Harmony Society of Pennsylvania where he was a follower. He purchased a remote stretch of land along the Saginaw Bay between Bay City and Caseville. For $25, people could join the colony named Ora Labora, after the Latin phrase "ora et labora" which means "pray and work". The colony started out with about 140 members and grew to about 280.

The first members of the colony came to the site and built log cabins. As more members came, they built a large lodge to use as a boarding house for the single men who moved to the colony. Work was exhausting as they worked Monday through Friday, from sunrise to sunset with an hour for lunch. Saturdays were for time with family and Sundays for worship.

Although the members were honest, hard working people, most were unskilled at farming, lumbering and construction. For instance, after purchasing cows and cattle, the livestock roamed away since the colony members did not know they needed fences. After building a 300-foot-long dock into Saginaw Bay one summer, it was destroyed by ice that same winter.

In 1862, some of the members became ill, and a little girl was the first to die. Incidentally, this was when the cemetery was established. Many of the male members joined the Michigan Militia to fight in the Civil War. After the war, most of them did not return to the colony. The colony received contracts to build telephone poles and railroad ties using the timber on their land. After incurring massive debt for supplies they had purchased, Ora Labora went into financial ruin. With only about twelve members remaining, the colony disbanded in 1867, and the property was divided up among themselves. The Great Fire of 1871 obliterated what was left of the colony, and all that remains are the tombstones of some of the former residents on the hill in the cemetery at the end of Sand Road.

Idlewild

The Casa Blanca Hotel

Location:
Idlewild Historic & Cultural Center
7025 S. Broadway Avenue
Idlewild, MI 49642
43.8872533, -85.7728497

Traveling down US-10 east of Baldwin in the Manistee National Forest, you may notice a sign for the town of Idlewild. If you stay on US-10, it may seem that Idlewild was a small town that is now mostly gone. If you turn off of the main highway, you will realize that Idlewild was a rather large community that has greatly diminished over the decades.

The town was started as a resort for African Americans in the early part of the 1900s. African Americans were limited to where they could vacation because of discrimination. Idlewild developers advertised to prominent black businessmen in cities like Detroit and Chicago. One of the earliest residents was African American Dr. Daniel Hale Williams, who successfully completed the first heart surgery in 1893. Over the decades, the resort town would blossom to thousands of residents, many of them traveling by train to vacation at their summer home. From 1912 through the mid-1960s, the area was known as the "Black Eden of Michigan".

The Flamingo Club sits near Idlewild Lake and opened in 1955 to entertain the growing number of people. It was a popular place for many of the top African American entertainers to perform, such as Aretha

The Flamingo Club

Franklin, Jackie Wilson, and The Four Tops. The pale green building sits empty, and the sound of music no longer permeates through its walls.

Strangely, the passage of the Civil Rights Act of 1964 doomed the popular tourist town. The popularity of Idlewild declined as African Americans now had the opportunity to purchase cottages and to vacation in other popular areas throughout the state. By 1968, the Flamingo Club had closed. The town was especially hard hit with the recession in the 1970s. Today, only a few houses remain on the many streets that made up the once thriving community. Among the houses is a large white and tan brick building. It was the Casa Blanca Hotel that closed down a long time ago. Efforts are underway to restore the old building.

The Idlewild Historic & Cultural Center is located at 7025 S Broadway St, Idlewild, MI 49642 and has information and displays about the historic resort community.

Port Crescent

Location:
Port Crescent State Park
1775 Port Austin Road (M-25)
Port Austin, MI 48467

Port Crescent Cemetery
Coordinates
44.0005315, -83.049742

Along M-25, a few miles from Port Austin, is an old iron bridge nestled among the trees that spans over a small mostly dried up creek. The sign hanging from the top beams reads: MICHIGAN BRIDGE AND PIPE CO. LANSING MICHIGAN. The bridge is one of the remnants of the forgotten port town of Port Crescent.

The town started in 1844 when Walter Hume built a hotel and trading post near the mouth of the Pinnebog River that empties into the Saginaw Bay. A few sawmills sprang up in the area around the river, and the town was known as Pinnebog, but another town upriver had the same name. A decision was made to change the name of the town to Port Crescent for the crescent shape of the river

near the mouth on the Saginaw Bay.

The lumber town flourished and even survived the Great Fire of 1871. Woods and Company built a large steam-powered sawmill with a brick smokestack that soared into the sky. The town had several houses and even built a large two-story schoolhouse to educate the children. By 1881, the lumberjacks had cut most of the timber, and any that were still standing was destroyed by The Great Fire that swept through the thumb. Slowly, houses and buildings were moved or dismantled and taken to surrounding towns such as Port Austin and Bad Axe. By 1894, most of the buildings were gone and very little remained of the once prosperous town.

Any trees large enough for lumber were gone, but a few people who remained in the town realized the sand in the area was valuable for glass making and copper smelting. They began a mining operation and shipped the sand to industries around the Great Lakes. By the 1930s, sand mining operations had ceased, and that would have been the end of the land being used for anything. After WWII, and the prosperity that followed, Michigan families began to vacation during the summer. The state of Michigan acquired the property along the shoreline in 1959 and established the Port Crescent State Park.

Little remains of the town of Port Crescent. The old bridge is used as part of a hiking trail, and the foundation for the sawmill chimney stands near the entrance to the campground. Next time you visit Port Crescent State Park or drive past the sign for it on M-25, maybe you will remember the town and the hard-working lumberjacks who lived there.

Port Crescent State Park has two entrances—a day use area and a campground entrance that is separated by a few miles. The old chimney foundation and bridge are near the campground entrance.

Dunes Forest Village

Dunes Forest Village circa 1960. Creative Commons Wikipedia

Location:
Silver Lake State Park
1765 N Lakeview Dr,
Mears, MI 49436

Swift Lathers Home and Museum
5809 W Fox Rd,
Mears, MI 49436
43.6817081, -86.4228907

People drive around on the sand dunes of Silver Lake
State Park in jeeps, quads, side x sides and dune
buggies. I bet few of the drivers know about the little

village that once stood on the dunes. Called Dunes Forest Village, it was built by eccentric local journalist Swift Lathers.

Lathers self published a newspaper he called *The Mears Newz* from the nearby town of Mears. He was well educated and graduated from University of Michigan Law School, but never took the bar exam or practiced law. He was a master of the English language, and he wrote many editorials speaking out for individual rights, the support of rural schools, and many other social causes. Charges were filed against him a few times to suppress what he published, but he successfully defended himself and the freedom of the press. One of the cases went all the way to the State Supreme Court, in which he successfully argued in his defense. He published his paper for fifty-six years until his death in 1970.

Swift homesteaded some land in 1939 in the dunes along Lake Michigan. Because of the sandy terrain, vehicles could not drive out to the spot in the dunes where a patch of trees grew. Lathers carried lumber and materials by hand to build small buildings the size of storage sheds in what he called Dunes Forest Village. Over the span of twenty years, he built a jail, schoolhouse and a chapel along with several other small houses and cabins. It was a little retreat for his friends and family.

Eventually, the land the village stood on became part of the state park. The buildings were all removed by the 1970s. If you know where to look, you might find some boards from one of Swift Lathers' buildings. Unfortunately, the exact location has been lost to time.

Swift Lathers' home in Mears is now a museum operated by the Oceana County Historical Society.

Iva and the Haunted Cemetery

Location:
Intersection of Iva and Dice Roads
near Hemlock.
43.4633183, -84.2695052

A cute light blue and white building that used to be a general store is about all that remains of the town of Iva, located a few miles northwest of Hemlock in Saginaw County. The post office in Iva opened December 7, 1894, with John F. Shovan as its first postmaster. The post office closed in October 1904.

About a mile east on Dice Road is an old cemetery. I am sure it is where some of the residents of Iva are laid to rest. The cemetery also has a reputation of being haunted. They say it is haunted by the ghost of a young girl. As the story goes, 5-year old Anna Rhodes Fazio was living in Italy in 1816 with her family when her father went insane and set their house on fire, killing himself and her mother. Young Anna survived the fire and sailed to America, and lived with her aunt in the area north of Hemlock. They became friends with the local Indians. Anna and a young Indian boy named Dark Hawk grew up together.

As Anna grew older, she fell in love with Jonathan Millerton, and they were married by the time Anna was 17. Shortly after they wed, Anna's aunt died, and Jonathan had to sail the Great Lakes for his lumbering pursuits, leaving Anna alone. Dark Hawk became jealous of Jonathan, and began to sexually assault Anna, driving her into insanity. That summer, a large storm swept across the state, and when Jonathan's ship did not return she feared him dead and committed suicide. Even more tragic, Jonathan returned home after she died; his ship had sailed to a few other ports and delayed his return.

If you visit the town of Iva, please be respectful. The old general store went out of business years ago, but it is still owned by someone. When visiting any cemetery, please follow the posted rules.

The general store was featured in a documentary by Haunted Saginaw.

McClure

Location:
The church in McClure
1194 McClure Rd,
Gladwin, MI 48624
44.03811240, -84.4163779

In the farmlands in the center of the state, northeast of Gladwin, stands an old church on a lonely dirt road where the people of the little lumber town of McClure worshiped. It's about all that remains of the town named after lumber baron William C. McClure, who built a sawmill in 1883. After the trees were cut down, it became a sleepy little farming community, and the church, which is now the Lighthouse Prayer Chapel, still marks the spot where the town once stood. I always think of how hard it must have been for the farmers to pull stumps from the fields. Before the giant hydraulic equipment we have today, it must have been extremely difficult backbreaking work.

Podunk

Location:
Intersection of N. Shearer and
Ziemer Roads. Near Gladwin
44.052656, -84.565298

Yes, there is a town in Michigan called Podunk. Actually, there are a couple of towns in a few different Michigan counties called Podunk. An old schoolhouse is a few miles northwest of Gladwin in the forgotten town of Podunk. I could not find any info about the town other than the name and location. I am guessing it was an old logging camp, but it's only a guess. I mostly liked the name. If you live in the center of the mitten and want to go for an afternoon drive, why not take a trip to Podunk? The schoolhouse sits on private property, but it is visible from the road.

Porter

Location:
2160 W Pine River Rd,
Breckenridge, MI 48615
43.53157692, -84.456285

Almost nothing remains of the town of Porter except for a few houses and an old service station. Michigan has or had a couple of towns named Porter, and this one is along the Pine River between Midland and St. Louis. It was given a post office in 1869, and then it closed a few decades later in 1907. If you travel along West Pine River Road, you may see the old gas station that people have told me was named Polly's Place.

West Pine River Road winds its way along the Pine River. It is a paved smooth road and is a popular road with motorcyclists.

Ghost Towns of the Big Farm

Old store in the Prarie Farms area of Saginaw County.

Location:
Old Prairie Saloon and store
5986 Fergus Rd,
St Charles, MI 48655
43.256137, -84.0313583

The land south of Saginaw between Birch Run and St. Charles is mostly farmland. At one time, it was part of the largest farm in Michigan. It supported a few small towns that are gone now, but the story of the farm is fascinating.

After the treaty of Saginaw in 1819 with the Chippewa Indians, the government acquired vast tracts of land. It sold the land to U.S. citizens for a low price of $100 for 80 acres to be used as farming. The marshy swampland south of Saginaw was not attractive for farming until Saginaw attorney Harland P. Smith and investors purchased 10,000 acres of the muddy wetland and named it Prairie Farm (maybe because Swamp Farm did not sound that appealing). They believed that if they could build dikes and ditches, they could drain the swamp and use the fertile ground to grow crops. The project proved too costly, and by the 1890s, they had sold out to the Wicks Brothers of Saginaw, who continued with digging drainage ditches and building dikes.

With the price of sugar rising because of the limited supply of sugar cane, sugar beets became a popular alternative, and Michigan was going through a sugar manufacturing boom. In 1903, the Owosso Sugar Co. bought Prairie Farm. Owosso Sugar was owned by the Pitcairn family, multimillionaire owners of the Pittsburgh Plate Glass Co, and they had the backing needed to complete the drainage work and cultivate most of the land. They built 36 miles of dikes to keep the land from flooding in the spring and also built a pump station on the Flint River, and a generator to supply power to the pumps and the farm.

During the early 1900s, many European immigrants came to work at the Prairie Farm, and by 1917, the farm was the largest farm east of the Mississippi. After World War I started and there were less immigrants from Europe, the farm began hiring Mexican immigrants. The farm's primary crop was sugar beets, but it also grew corn,

A row of workers' shacks at Prarie Farms early 1900s

wheat, soy beans and peppermint. The farm also raised sheep and pigs. Overproduction of crops and economic decline caused the Owosso Sugar Co. to go out of business in 1928.

In 1933, Russian immigrant and newspaper editor Joseph J. Cohen purchased the farm to start a self-sustaining farming commune and called it Sunrise Cooperative Farm Community. To join the commune, families had to give the co-op farm a non refundable $1000, and they lived and worked on the farm. All land and property was owned by the community. The problem the community had was the people joining the commune were city folks with little farming knowledge. They soon had to hire experienced farm hands and took on large amounts of debt to pay the workers. They managed to get by for a few years, but in 1935 the crops were destroyed by an army worm infestation.

In December 1936, the cooperative sold Prairie Farm to the Federal Rural Rehabilitation Corp, a "New Deal" agency established to revive the agricultural sector. Sunrise briefly operated the farm as a government tenant, but by

January 1937, there were only 25 families left. In 1945, the federal government sold Prairie Farm to an association that subsequently divided the land into parcels and sold them to private farmers.

One of the main towns the Prairie Farms created was the town of Alicia on the corner of Alicia and Bishop Roads in Saginaw County. It was the largest town in the Prairie Farm and was named after William Lewis Clause's oldest daughter. Mr. Clause was the chairman of the board of Pittsburgh Plate Glass, who owned the farm at that time. It was where most of the hired workers and their foremen lived. A generator and water plant provided electricity and water to the town that included 80 yellow framed cottages, a general store, a boarding house, dance hall, and several large barns and other buildings for machinery and wagons. The population would grow to about 350 workers in the summer, and then about 75 in the winter. The post office opened in 1904 and closed in 1947. Today it has some modern houses and an old barn, but I am not sure if they were used during the time that Prairie Farm operated.

Another town is the town of Clausedale. It is gone and the only thing around is a dirt road bearing its name. The town was named after William Lewis Clause, who was the president of Pittsburgh Plate and Glass Company that invested in the Prairie Farm in central Saginaw County. Clausedale was the center of the sheep operations and where the workers who raised and sheared the sheep lived. When the Prairie Farm ended operations in the town of Clausedale ended with it.

On the corner of Fergus and Bishop Roads in Albee Township across from the old Prairie Saloon, (now Good Times) sits an old general store-looking building. According to an old plot map, this was known as McDonough or Mcdonough Corners. There was a post office that operated there from 1892 to 1903. I wonder if this is where the workers went to get a drink; hence, the Prairie Saloon.

The Big School House in Fern

Location:
The old Fern school
6005 S Custer Rd,
Custer, MI 49405
43.84652, -86.2187761

The ruins of this two-story schoolhouse stand along the road in rural Mason County watching the farmers work the fields. Above the entrance is a carved stone that reads: FERN SCHOOL DIST. 3 1906. It's all that remains of the town of Fern.

The town was built around a sawmill owned by J.S. Adams in Eden Township. A station was built on the Mason and

Oceana Railroad in 1886, and two years later it was given a post office. I am not sure why it was named Fern, but the town must have prospered to build a two-story brick schoolhouse, considering most of the school houses I see left standing are simple single-story wooden structures. A year after the school was built, the town's post office closed, probably because the postal system went to rural free delivery where they would deliver to every house and residence instead of residents having to pick up their mail at the post office. After the timber was gone, the mill must have closed along with the train depot, since there are no longer any tracks running near the old forgotten school. The school closed in 1959, and it stands eerily empty, remembering the days when the children of Fern came to visit.

> Please note. Enjoy these old forgotten places from the road; be respectful and do not trespass.

Nirvana

Location:
Nirvana Cemetery
East Knight Street
Chase, MI 49623
43.9015646, -85.7277660

The town of Nirvana was off US-10 west of Reed City. It was originally platted by Darwin Knight, who became the town's first postmaster in 1874. He built the town near the Flint & Pere Marquette Railroad. I am not sure if Mr. Knight was Buddhist, but he must have been fond of its beliefs. He gave the town the name of Nirvana, which is the name of Buddhist highest heaven. He named the town's hotel The Indra House, after Indra, the principal god of the Ayran-Vedic religion. When timber was king, eleven sawmills operated in the town. But like most of the towns in the area, once the timber was all cut down, the sawmills moved, along with the people who worked at them.

Other than some of the people resting in peace in the local cemetery, I am thinking nothing remains from Nirvana's timbering days. At one time, there was a sign for Nirvana, but it was stolen a few times, probably by fans of the Seattle grunge band of the same name. After replacing the sign a few times, it was decided it was not worth replacing anymore.

Forgotten Town of Hamlin

Location:
Ludington State Park
8800 M-116
Ludington, MI 49431

Hamlin Cemetery
44.0352300, -86.4942508

The remains of the sawmill town of Hamlin are one of the most visited places by tourists in Michigan. The strange thing is, most people don't even know they have visited it.

In the 1850s, lumberman Charles Mears purchased large tracts of land around the Ludington area for timber. About ten miles north of present day Ludington, the Big Sable River flows into Lake Michigan. This is where Mears constructed a wooden dam in order to create a holding pond for logs waiting to be cut at the sawmill, which was powered by the dam. Shipping docks were built out into Lake Michigan so ships could load the enormous amounts of lumber cut in the mill. As workers began to relocate to the profitable mill, a town grew around it. Mears gave the town the name of Big Sable. A few years earlier, he constructed a mill a couple miles south on Black Creek that was named Little Sable. After the election of Abraham Lincoln, Mears changed the name of Little Sable to Lincoln to honor the sixteenth president. Big Sable was renamed Hamlin in honor of Lincoln's Vice President Hannibal Hamlin.

The town of Hamlin prospered for several years until 1888, when the wooden dam broke, destroying most of the village. Fortunately, no lives were lost in the disaster, but both the dam and town had to be rebuilt. The new dam lasted until 1912, when it also failed. The rushing water once again whipped most of the town out into Lake Michigan. The sawmill and town were never reconstructed, but a new dam was built. The pond, now named Lake Hamlin, was no longer used for holding logs but many houses were built along its shoreline. The new dam restored the lake so it could be used for recreation and enjoyed by fisherman and kayakers to this day.

In the 1930s, the Civilian Conservation Corps developed the area into Ludington State Park. The popularity of the park draws in thousands of visitors every year. It is one of Michigan's most popular state parks, but I wonder how many know of the sawmill town that once stood along the river. A hiking trail along the river has some remnants and artifacts from the old town.

In the woods, on a hill near the northwest corner of the Hamlin Lake beach parking lot, is the old cemetery where some of the residents of Hamlin are laid to rest.

Chapter Three
Northern Lower Peninsula

Aral and the Hanging Tree

Location:
On the shoreline of Lake
Michigan at the end of Esch Rd.
off M-22 a few miles south of
Empire.
44.7627963, -86.073618

Started in the 1880s, the town of Aral was a small
lumbering community near Empire on the shores of Lake
Michigan. Charles Wright managed the sawmill and was
known for his short temper and willingness to fight

anyone who crossed him. In August 1889, the sheriff sent a deputy and treasurer to collect on taxes the sawmill owed to the county. Mr. Wright met the two men as they came into town, and after a short argument he shot and killed both of them, leaving their bodies in the street.

He went back to work at the sawmill as if nothing happened. Wright must have gotten word from someone that a telegraph message was sent back to the sheriff about the violent murder of the two men. Charles Wright shut down operations for the day and then disappeared into the nearby forest. When the sheriff and a posse of twenty men showed up in the little town of Aral, they found Wright's Native American handyman Peter Lahala.

The posse tied a rope around the Indian's neck and threw it over a nearby tree. They pulled him up for a few minutes and then lowered him back down, trying to get him to disclose the whereabouts of Charles Wright. At the start of hoisting Lahala for a third time, two men marched Charles Wright out of the woods, and he was taken into custody. He was convicted of murder and sentenced to prison for the rest of his life. While he served his sentence, he worked as a bookkeeper in the

The Sawmill in Aral late 1800s

prison's office. Wright served only ten years because his sentence was commuted by Michigan Governor Hazen S. Pingree. To this day, no one knows why the governor released him from prison early.

After the deadly events, the tree in town became forever known as "the hanging tree". The town continued to thrive until the timber was gone. The population slowly dwindled, and by the 1920s, all the buildings and houses had been moved away.

The former town's location is in the Sleeping Bear Dunes National Lakeshore. Near Esch Beach is a sign describing the forgotten town of Aral. An old tree lies nearby, and many say that is the remains of the infamous hanging tree.

Bell's Ghost Town Chimney

Location:
Location: Besser Natural Area on
Besser Bell Road near
12057 E Grand Lake Rd.
Presque Isle, MI 49777
Chimney 45.2501449, -83.4149891
Cemetery 45.24502, -83.41732

The ghost town of Bell sits in the Besser Natural Area
and is open to hikers. A one mile loop traverses the
wilderness and along the path remains of the forgotten
town can be seen. A large stone chimney stands tall,

marking the spot where the little logging town once stood. Along with the chimney, there are a few walls of an old general store and a broken safe lying nearby. I found several artifacts lying on the ground, like bits of metal and old cans. Hopefully, visitors will be kind enough to look at them and then leave them for other explorers like I did.

The village grew around the Presque Isle Brick and Lumber Company. The post office opened in 1884 in what I assume was the general store that you find in pieces today. The post office closed in 1911.

West of the parking lot is an overgrown two track trail that heads due west into the trees. If you walk down the trail for about one hundred yards, you will find the old Bell Cemetery. It is surrounded by a wooden picket fence. It is an interesting little cemetery with headstones made out of concrete. Since Alpena is the cement capitol of Michigan, it makes sense that the tombstones would be made out of concrete.

If you visit, be sure to take some bug spray. When I hiked the trail in the spring, the mosquitoes were so thick they could have carried me away.

Middle Village

Location:
101 N Lamkin Rd,
Harbor Springs, MI 49740
45.5520435, -85.1152849

Thousands of motorists travel down M-119 through the "tunnel of trees" between Harbor Springs and Coss Village. A popular stop is the general store in Good Hart. The town of Middle Village sits between Good Hart and Lake Michigan. It can be a little tricky to find, but if you turn onto Lamkin Road near the Good Hart General Store, it will take you back to the village.

Originally called Apatawaaing by the Native Americans, Middle Village became a Jesuit Mission in 1823. Among the summer cottages are a couple of old log cabins that stand next to the road. St Ignatius Church also stands in the village, and next to it is a graveyard with white wooden crosses of the residents who died long ago.

Next to the church is a trail that leads to Middle Village Par Beach on Lake Michigan. The park also has an overlook that is open all year long and is a wonderful place to watch a sunset.

Lamkin Road south of Middle Village becomes narrow and steep; it's recommended that you come in from Good Hart and head back out that direction.

Duncan and the Lighthouse Ruins

Location:
Lighthouse Ruins inside the
Cheboygan State Park
4490 Beach Road
Cheboygan, MI 49721
Ruins are located at
45.66896420, -84.41972027

Duncan Bay is located east of where the Cheboygan River flows into Lake Huron. In the early 1800s, the Cheboygan River was too shallow for ships to sail up into it, and Duncan Bay was deep and allowed for ships to safely sail into it. On the western side of the bay is where Duncan

City once stood. It was named after Jeremiah Duncan, who started lumbering in the area. The city was a company town in its heyday with a population of about 500 and was named the county seat when Cheboygan County was created. Jeremiah Duncan began constructing a new sawmill in 1852 but died shortly after. The town's popularity dwindled, and the county seat was moved to Cheboygan in 1856.

Duncan City began to struggle more when the Cheboygan River was dredged out deeper, thus allowing more shipping traffic to go to Cheboygan itself. The final blow for Duncan City came in 1898 when the sawmill burned to the ground.

A private marina and houses are located where the city once stood. Duncan Road leads out to the marina and is the only reminder in the area of the once booming sawmill town.

Although the remnants of Duncan City are gone, across the bay in Cheboygan State Park is the foundation of the old Cheboygan Point Lighthouse. Built in 1859, the lighthouse was constructed to guide ships around Lake Huron and into Duncan Bay. After the Fourteen Foot Shoal Lighthouse was constructed off shore in 1930, the old lighthouse was no longer needed. The land was given to the state for the creation of the state park. Unfortunately, vandals damaged the old lighthouse and it was dismantled for the lumber. The foundation remained like a tombstone for the old lighthouse whose light guided sailors around the Great Lakes.

A trail in Cheboygan State Park takes hikers past the ruins of the old lighthouse.

Alabaster and the Loading Dock

Loading dock in Lake Huron demolished in 2020

Location of Historical Marker:
3005 Benson Rd,
Tawas City, MI 48763
44.19244859, -83.5561329

South of Tawas on US-23 is an area next to Lake Huron that has white sections of land. It looks like white sand, but it is actually alabaster gypsum. Originally mined for fertilizer and plaster, it is an ingredient in drywall; in some parts of the country it's called sheetrock.

Mining began in the 1840s, and by 1864, people living in the area became a large enough community to be given a post office with the town being named Alabaster.

The mine grew to become one of the nation's top-producing gypsum mines by the late 1800s. A fire in 1891 destroyed most of the mine's buildings, but it was rebuilt in time to supply material for the 1893 Chicago Columbian Exposition. It is also known as the "World's Fair", and it had ornate buildings, with marble-like walls made from plaster earning it the title of "The White City". The buildings were made with plaster because they were designed to be temporary structures and torn down after the exposition.

In 1902, the mine was incorporated as the U.S. Gypsum Corporation and the company built housing for its workers. As the demand for alabaster gypsum grew, so did the town. It had three churches, a blacksmith shop and a

Postcard of Alabaster 1910

wagon maker. The demand for gypsum grew, and to aid in the loading of ships, an elevated marine tramway was constructed in 1928 and stretched 1.3 miles out into the Saginaw Bay. Like a horizontal ski-lift, the cable system carried 72 "buckets" of gypsum to a waiting ship or to the storage bin in the loading building. Each bucket held more than two tons. The tramway included 6,450 feet of one and three-quarter inch steel cable and 14,000 feet of three-quarter inch cable. At a length of 6,350 feet, it was the longest over-water bucket tramway in the world.

Mining slowed in the middle of the 20th century, and the post office closed in 1962. Eventually, everyone moved away and all the buildings were demolished. The tramway was demolished in the 1990s, and the offshore loading dock building was razed in 2020. A road leads into the area where the town once stood, but it is gated off because the area is still being mined. A historical marker stands next to Lake Huron in memory of the town, and a little church is not far away. I can only assume it was where some of the citizens of Alabaster worshiped when the town was prosperous.

Pere Cheney

Location of Historical Marker:
Center Plains Trail between
Grayling and Roscommon
Cemetery: 44.57333, -84.6351629
Townsite: 44.578970, -84.6394417

Before Grayling was the county seat of Crawford County, one of the largest towns in the area was Pere Cheney. It was a lumbering town established in 1874 by George Cheney, who received a land grant from the Michigan Central Railroad. The population grew to about 1500 people and included a general store, railroad depot, post office, sawmill and hotel with telegraph service. Sadly, in 1893, diphtheria spread throughout the village, killing most of its citizens. In 1897, diphtheria returned, and by 1917, there were only eighteen people left in the town, so it was sold off in an auction. Since then, all the buildings have disappeared, and only a cemetery remains, about a mile south of where the town once stood.

Because of the tragic demise of the town, rumors began to spread that it was built on an old Indian burial ground. Another rumor is that a witch cast a curse on the town after being banished into the nearby woods. There are reports of lights in the woods, and they say you can hear children playing, and sometimes they leave handprints on the car when you visit. Only a few headstones remain in the graveyard, and many are broken or have fallen over. But that does not stop visitors from leaving flowers and coins.

Where the town once stood are some depressions in the ground that mark where the buildings once stood. It's rather secluded, and it is strange to see a cemetery in the middle of the woods. If I hadn't known it was there, and I had come across it by accident, it would have really spooked me!

If you want to find the old cemetery, don't rely on your GPS. It will take you down some nearly impassable forest roads. The best way to go is to take 4 Mile Road a few miles east of I-75 and head south down Beasley Avenue about a mile and a half. It will curve southeast into East Railroad Trail and follow along the railroad tracks. Travel about a mile, and then there will be a road that crosses over the tracks. After crossing the tracks, turn left onto Center Plains Trail and about a half mile down will be the old cemetery. I recommend having an all-wheel drive vehicle as the roads are sandy and also get muddy when they are wet.

The town once stood just north of where you cross the railroad tracks to get to the cemetery.

Big Rock

Location:
8036 M-32
Atlanta, MI 49709
45.0069315, -84.2340660

It is said that when an iceberg is floating in the ocean, you can only see about ten percent of it sticking out of the water. That is also the case for a giant boulder that is sticking out of the ground in northern Michigan. No one knows exactly how large the "big rock" is, but it can be seen on M-32 between Gaylord and Atlanta.

In 1882, Seth Gillet became the first postmaster for the town named after the geological feature. By 1902, a general store owned by Briley Township pioneer William Remington housed the post office. The town continued to grow, and a church, school, hall, sawmill and a blacksmith shop were also located in Big Rock. As the timber in the area declined, so did the population of the town, and the post office officially closed in 1920. Nothing remains from the old forgotten town except the rock and a couple of signs for people to read if they are willing to stop and learn more.

Store owner Charles Harrison tried to dig up the big rock and put it on display in 1940. He was only able to dig a tunnel under it and gave up.

Onominese

Location:
9637 N. Onominese Trail
Northport, MI 49670
45.1225039, -85.6667883

Rows of white wooden crosses stand in a simple cemetery near Lake Michigan. The people laid to rest are all that remains of the small Indian village of Onominese. The village was named after the Native American Chief Onominese (also spelled Onominee) and was about five miles north of Leland on the Leelanau Peninsula.

For generations, a tribe of Ottawa and Chippewa migrated from lower Michigan to the Leelenau area in the summer. The people who lived there generally traveled to the town by canoe as there were no roads leading to the village. Reverend George N. Smith did missionary work with the Native Americans for about a decade in southern Michigan and gained their respect and trust. After moving to Northport, Reverend Smith convinced the Native Americans to stay permanently instead of using the location as a temporary summer village.

Reverend Smith traveled from Northport every Sunday through crude forest trails to conduct church services. After the Civil War ended in 1865, a small schoolhouse was built to teach the children from seven to seventeen. Besides bringing Christianity and education to the Native Americans, the white man also brought an epidemic of smallpox and diphtheria that killed most of the small village's population. If the white crosses standing in the field near Lake Michigan could talk, they would tell the story of the people who died in the small forgotten village.

Access to the cemetery is limited because it is on a private road for the nearby houses.

Deward and the Sawmill

Ruins of the old Deward sawmill.

Location:
Off N. Manistee River Rd.
Frederic, MI 49733
44.836173, -84.836904

The town of Deward started with the death of David Ward, one of Michigan's wealthiest lumber barons. Upon his death in 1900, he left his vast timber lands to his six children with the provision that the profits be divided up twelve years after his death. His sons built a massive state

93

of the art sawmill along the Manistee River, northwest of Grayling. Ward's sons had their father's name "D.WARD" painted on the side of the mill. As lumberjacks and mill workers began moving to the area to work at the mill, they just began calling the town Deward for the name painted on the mill.

The town quickly grew to have over eight hundred residents with boarding houses, a general store, a church and a community center, but no bar because alcohol was prohibited. The lumberjacks fed trees into the monster of a sawmill as fast as they could before the twelve years expired, as specified in Ward's will. In that short time, the area was stripped of all the trees, which were cut into boards. The sawmill closed in 1912, and the town died

The old sawmill in Deward

off. The buildings were dismantled and hauled away, and the old sawmill was demolished, but some concrete foundations remain.

The best way to find the ruins is from County Road 612. Take Manistee River Road north. About a mile and a half north of West Cameron Bridge Road, you will see a two-track heading west with a small green sign with a binoculars symbol on it. Go down that road about 100 yards to a parking area. Take the trail down to the river. You will see an old wooden fence with concrete bases at each end which are left over from the sawmill. From the south base, head into the woods about fifty yards and you will see the concrete foundations. You can't miss them, they are huge, about the size of a pickup truck. The threaded rods sticking out of the top are about two or three inches in diameter. Whatever was mounted to them must have been massive.

Do not rely on your GPS as it may take you down two track trails that are not suitable for a truck. I know this because that is what happened to me on my first trip to find the old ghost town. During the summer, you can get there in a car, but I would recommend a truck or SUV, especially in the spring and fall when it is raining a lot.

Harlan

Location:
15300 Harlan Rd,
Copemish, MI 49625
44.4580116, -85.81875972

This old church stands quietly in the town of Harlan located in northern Michigan east of Copemish. In the 1880s, the railroad was originally going to go through the nearby town of Cleon. Because of the steep grades and sharp curves, they decided to run through the town of

Harlan instead. It gave the town a boost in population. Having several stores, a blacksmith shop, and a hotel, the town prospered until the railroad no longer stopped in the little town. By the 1950s, most of the businesses had closed. Not much remains in Harlan but an old church and a few houses.

Glen Haven

Location:
5121 Glen Haven Rd,
Glen Arbor, MI 49636
44.9032117, -86.027238

The village of Glen Haven is a few miles west of Glen Arbor in the Sleeping Bear Dunes. The town started out in 1857 when C. C. McCarty built a sawmill and inn next to the beach. After the Civil War, the town was purchased by the Northern Transit Company, they built a dock, and the town was the primary place for their twenty-four ships to load up on firewood to fuel the steam engines. As passenger ships docked for fuel, people would get off and visit, and the little town became somewhat of a resort town.

In 1878, D.H. Day was selected by the Northern Transit Company to be the town's agent and manage its daily affairs. Day put his savvy business skills to use and built a railway to haul logs into town and tourists away from town. By the beginning of the 1900s, most ships used coal for fuel and passenger service declined because it was easier to take the train.

In 1920, D.H. Day built the Glen Haven Canning Company for canning cherries and apples he grew in his orchards. In 1935, Day's daughter Marion and her husband Luis Warnes purchased a 1934 Ford and gave passengers rides on the dunes for twenty-five cents. They operated out of the Sleeping Bear Inn, and by the time the rides ended in 1978, there were 13 "dunesmobiles", each carrying 14 passengers on a 12-mile, 35-minute excursion.

By the mid 1970s, the National Park Service had taken over the little town and restored the blacksmith shop and general store. The old cannery is now used as a maritime museum. During the winter months, it is rather quiet, but in the summer, it is bustling with tourists exploring and learning about days gone by.

Afton

Location:
259 M-68,
Afton, MI 49705
45.37391, -84.4922473
Private Property but visible from
the road.

Located between Indian River and Onaway on M-68, many people passed through the town of Afton. It may not be a true ghost town since there are a few houses and a beautiful little church still in the area, but the row of old abandoned buildings sure makes it feel like a ghost town. Afton started as a lumber camp in 1887. In 1905, it was given a post office. The nearby Pigeon River was similar to the Afton River in Scotland, and thus the town was named after it. Over the years, the town's population has declined to a handful of people that it is today.

Sauble

Location:
9976 W 3 Mile Rd,
Branch Township, MI 49402
44.0325096, -85.9988434

An old log cabin stands in the Huron Manistee National forest about 15 miles northwest of Baldwin. The hand-painted sign above the door reads: "Sauble Station est 1937". The town started in 1898 with a depot on the Manistee and Grand Rapids Railroad. A post office was opened up in the general store in 1910. I could not find anything that tells the story of the demise of the small sawmill town, but I can only assume the trees were cut by the lumberjacks. With no trees left for cutting up into lumber, the lumberjacks moved on and the town faded away.

A little log cabin stands along the road where the town once stood. A long time ago, it was a service station selling gas to local motorists. I am not sure if it is old enough to have been part of the original town, but it is a reminder of the long-forgotten town in the western Michigan forest.

Star City

Location:
Star City Cemetery
1879 N Star City Rd,
Lake City, MI 49651
Old Schoolhouse (Privately Owned)
44.37235618, -84.984156

I love the name Star City. It sounds like a promising place full of celebrities with glitz and glamor. In reality, it is or was in the middle of nowhere west of Houghton Lake in the center of the Mitten. An old schoolhouse and cemetery are all that remains of the town. I found a couple of different references to it, but I am not sure how accurate they are.

One story I found claimed that Star City was originally named Starvation Lake after a local trapper who was found dead in his cabin from starvation. In an attempt to sell property for farming and hunting around the small city, developers renamed the area Star Lake. Unfortunately, the name change did not help, and the developers went bankrupt. Eventually, people began referring to the small town as Star City.

The other reference I found says that the settlement dates from approximately 1872. A post office named "Roy" opened February 27, 1880, with Chauncey Brace as the first postmaster. The name changed to "Putnam" on June 6, 1883, with Elizabeth Putnam as postmaster. The name changed again to "Star City" on February 13, 1885 and was discontinued on December 15, 1923.

Whichever is true, the town is mostly forgotten now. This old schoolhouse knows the story, but unfortunately, walls don't talk.

North Unity

Location:
Old Log Cabin
1071 W Harbor Hwy,
Maple City, MI 49664
44.9216096, -85.8744774

Old Schoolhouse
44.9335289, -85.9081433

In the 1850s, with the lack of work in Chicago, some Bohemian (present-day Czech Republic) and German immigrants left the city and sailed Lake Michigan looking for paradise. They landed in Good Harbor in the Leelanau

Peninsula. After trekking about 10 miles inland, they found a beautiful piece of land to establish a new community they called North Unity. With the spread of typhoid throughout Chicago, their family and friends departed in October to start a new town in Northern Michigan. With winter coming, they decided to build a large 150-foot long barrack. It was divided up inside with walls to house each family until they could build houses and establish farms in the spring.

The first winter was extremely challenging for the group. They had brought little supplies with them, and because of the winter, they were not able to grow food to feed their families. The local ponds and lakes were frozen over and they could not fish either. They purchased some corn from the local Indians and managed to keep off starving to death in time for the spring thaw.

In the spring, they built permanent houses and farms, and over the next few years, the little community began to prosper. Other people began moving to the little town in the Leelanau Peninsula. Eventually, a schoolhouse and a gristmill were constructed, and John Shalda built a general store. Sadly, in 1871, forest fires swept through Michigan and with it destroyed most of the buildings and houses of North Unity.

The people of the devastated community moved further inland to the area near the corner of M-22 and Bohemian Road. (County Road 669) They started a new community and built new houses and other buildings, including a church. John Shalda built a new general store and a log cabin. Not far away a new school was constructed. Most of the buildings are gone, and nothing remains of the original site of North Unity. The log cabin John Shalda constructed and the old log schoolhouse can still be seen today along M-22.

Damon

Approximate Location:
4915 N Fairview Rd,
West Branch, MI 48661
Cemetery 44.463955, -84.2284076

Not much remains of the town of Damon but an old general store and a few houses. Located about 10 miles north of West Branch, the town was first settled in 1878 and named for George Damon, owner of the firm Cutting & Damon. In the late 1800s, it was a booming lumbering town with a hotel and school for the children of the lumberjacks. It was given a post office in 1880, and the stagecoach stopped in the little town, dropping off mail and passengers, As the timber declined, so did the population, and the post office closed in 1907. The post office was briefly reopened in 1911 but closed two years later in 1915. Most of the buildings are gone except a little building with a sign that reads "Damon General Store".

The town was the inspiration for the town in Owosso author James Oliver Curwood's book *Green Timber.*

Coopersville

Location:
1860 Fire Tower Road
Lewiston, MI 49756
44.736311, -84.35414242

In the woods of northern Michigan is an old wild west town. You will not find it on a map since it was never an official town. The town of Coopersville (not to be confused with Coopersville near Grand Rapids) was built out of love by one man's passion for John Wayne and the wild west.

Spike Cooper constructed his town to look like a wild west movie set. It has a saloon, jail, general store, livery and more. The buildings are full of interesting antiques and funny signs adorning the exterior of the buildings. Spike welcomed visitors to explore his little town and share his passion for the old west.

Sadly, Spike Cooper passed away in 2020. His friends and family maintain the old western town of Coopersville and still welcome visitors.

It's not far from Hartwick Pines State Park and would be a good place to check out along with the logging museum and chapel at the state park.

Chapter Four
Upper Peninsula

The Ruins in Cliff

Cliff mine ruins off Cliff Drive.

Location:
Cliff Drive about 5 miles
north of Allouez
near Cliff Dr, Allouez, MI 49805
47.37201255, -88.3128432

Ruins approximately
47.37247968, -88.314929

Cliff Catholic Cemetery off US-41
47.367137, -88.307801

Deep in the forests north of Mohawk in the center of the Keweenaw Peninsula are the stone ruins of a once prosperous mine and town that supported it. The Cliff Mine is the first successful mine in the Michigan Copper District. Legend has it that copper was discovered in 1845 when a prospector was exploring the area and fell off the cliff. He injured his derriere—or, as Forrest Gump would say, "buttocks"—on a piece of protruding copper. The highly successful mine was the largest copper mine in the US for more than a decade after it was started. By the 1870s, the veins of copper had been extracted from the ground and the mine closed.

You can still see the stone walls and foundations from the buildings among the trees behind the tailings (piles of rocks) dug out from the mine. I was amazed by the stone tower that I am thinking was a chimney. You can find the old Cliff Mine ruins hiking over the west branch of the Eagle River off Cliff Drive where it connects back to US-41. When I visited, I parked by the roadside wooden sign for the town. A board was laid across a narrow part of the river where I could cross without getting my feet wet. You might have to walk up and down the river a little to find a good place to cross. I recommend going in the summer when it is dry and the river is low.

Church foundation ruins in the Catholic cemetery.

On US-41 is a sign for the Cliff Cemetery. The sign seems out of place because you cannot see a cemetery. The cemetery does exist, but it is hidden in the woods. After hiking about fifty yards into the forest, you will see tombstones standing quietly among the trees. The ground is covered by green leafy plants, which I think is wintergreen. Paths snake through the thick growth to the various grave sites.

In the back of the cemetery is an old stone foundation left over from the chapel that once stood next to the tombstones. The cemetery is from the town of Cliff. Two churches were constructed, one Catholic and the other Protestant, each with its own cemetery. The one next to

US-41 is the Catholic Cemetery. The Protestant Cemetery can be found off an overgrown two track seasonal road on Cliff Drive.

It is believed that the church in the nearby town of Phoenix once stood on the stone foundation in the Catholic cemetery.

Pequaming

Location:
Ford Dr.
L'Anse, MI 49946
Cemetery 46.8528844, -88.3949530

North of L'Anse on the Keweenaw Bay is a point that creates a natural harbor. The Ojibwe Indians had a settlement on the point called Pequaming. In the Ojibwe language, Pequaming means "headlands". In 1877, Charles Hebard and Edward Thurber purchased large tracts of land in the area and built a sawmill in Pequaming. Shortly after the company was formed, Thurber sold his half to Hebard. With the help of his sons, Charles Hebard's company became one of the largest sawmills in the Upper Peninsula. At its peak, they employed about a thousand workers and produced thirty million board feet of lumber per year.

After Charles Heberd died in 1904, his sons inherited the company. They had great success in the lumbering business, and in 1913 built a summer home in Pequaming known as "the bungalow."

Ford sawmill circa 1920

Former Odd Fellows hall near the Pequaming Cemetery

Ford Motor Company approached the brothers in 1922 about purchasing land for timber to produce wood parts for the Model T. The brothers convinced Henry Ford to purchase their whole operation for 2.8 million dollars. Ford purchased the sawmill and most of the buildings in the town and used the bungalow as his summer home.

Pequaming became a company town, and Ford used it as a model community for his beliefs on self-reliance and education. He built new schools for the workers' children, and his summer home was used for vocational training during the winter. With increased shipping costs, and the fact that wood was used less in the manufacturing of automobiles, Ford shut down the mill in 1942. The town slowly declined over the years, and most of the mill is gone. The brick powerhouse building remains along with the water tower that still has the Ford logo painted on it. The bungalow also stands along the bay and is privately owned but can be rented for various occasions.

Fiborn Quarry

Location:
Fiborn Quarry Road about 3 miles
north of Trout Lake Road
46.206104, -85.169110

Ruins 46.20618326, -85.1771253

Enormous concrete buildings stand quietly desolate in a remote part of the Upper Peninsula. In the isolated forests east of Trout Lake and north of Caffey, unusually pure limestone was discovered. Chase Osborn purchased the land, and with the help of Duluth, South Shore and

Atlantic Railroad president William Foresman Fitch, they formed the Fiborn Quarry. The name came from a combination of their last names. In 1904, after Fitch ran a spur line to the area, buildings and a crushing plant were constructed with supplies that were transported by the railroad.

At its peak, The Fiborn Limestone Co. had two locomotives and seventy-five people who worked for the quarry. Since there were so many employees and the Quarry was in a remote location, a town was constructed for the workers. In the beginning, employees stayed in the boarding houses while their families lived in nearby towns. Eventually, a road was constructed to the quarry and it became accessible by early automobiles such as Ford's Model-T. Families began moving to the town, and an elementary school was built to accommodate the children.

Getting limestone out of the ground and onto railroad cars was dangerous work. Dynamite was used to blast the rock into smaller pieces, and in December 1910, two workers died while setting dynamite into the limestone.

About a year later, a boiler in the crushing plant exploded, killing one worker and injuring seven others. Despite the dangers and challenges, the quarry was profitable until the Great Depression. In the 1930s, struggling industries no longer needed the limestone, and the quarry officially closed in 1936.

The buildings for the town as well as the railroad tracks to it are gone. Some of the concrete buildings remain. Like Greek or Roman ruins, they still stand among a strange looking landscape left from the quarrying of the limestone. The ruins are now part of the Karst Preserve which lies between St. Ignace and Newberry. They are open to the public. It is about a half mile hike to the buildings from the parking area. It is not a difficult hike, but it is in a remote area so be sure to bring some water, especially if it is a hot day in the summer.

The Haunted Ghost Town of Shelldrake

Location:
About 2 miles north of Paradise on private property not accessible to the public

Whitefish Point sticks out into Lake Superior in Michigan's Upper Peninsula. The town of Shelldrake, named after a duck common in the area, is a ghost town at the mouth of the Shelldrake River on Whitefish Point.

By the late 1890s, Shelldrake had a sawmill, houses, a hospital, a schoolhouse, a post office, and an icehouse that could store enough meat to feed a population of 1,000 through the winter months. The homes of the workers were even equipped with bathrooms; it was rare to have indoor plumbing in northern Michigan in those days.

Stories claim that the area is haunted by an old sea captain who stands on the dock near Shelldrake. He has a pipe and a cape, and he is usually seen from the lake. As boats approach the shore, he fades away and disappears. The tugboat Grace, which was towing a barge in October of 1879 through Whitefish Bay, was headed for Goulais Bay in Canada. During a storm in the early morning, the tugboat broke down and drifted onto a sandbar about 200 feet offshore from Shelldrake. The tug filled with water and broke into pieces. The crew made it to shore, and after climbing the bank to safety, the captain proclaimed, "Thank God, we are all safe", and then suddenly dropped dead of a heart attack. This may be the captain's ghost that has been seen on the docks.

In the early 1900s, the town's logging years on the Tahquamenon River peaked. By the 1920s, repeated fires and the decline of lumbering led to its demise. Today, it is a privately-owned ghost town with only a few weathered, original buildings. Unfortunately, it is closed to the public and it is not visible from the road.

Ford's Sawmill Town of Alberta

Location:
21235 Alberta Ave # 2
L'Anse, MI 49946
46.644175, -88.480305

Henry Ford was obsessed with building the Model-T as efficiently and inexpensive as possible. To do that, he used the process of vertical integration. Ford Motor Company created companies that supplied the factory with materials. Ford made their own steel, harvested rubber and built sawmills to supply lumber to the factory.

A few miles south of L'Anse on US-41 is the town of Alberta, where Henry Ford built a sawmill town in 1936 to supply lumber to his growing auto company. The town was named after the daughter of one of his executives. The community consisted of a sawmill, houses for the workers and their families, and two schools to educate the children while their parents were working. In 1954, the town of Alberta was donated to Michigan Tech and is still used today for forestry education. If you're in the area, they give tours of the historic town and sawmill to visitors.

Assinins

Orphanage ruins

Location:
Assinins Road L'Anse Twp, MI
46.81094056, -88.4759136

North of Baraga, on the shores of the Keweenaw Bay is what remains of the town of Assinins. The town was one of the earliest settlements in the region. Bishop Frederic Baraga frequently did missionary work with the local

127

Native Americans in the Upper Peninsula. He was invited to visit the area along the Keweenaw Bay by Chief Edward Assinins. In 1843, Bishop Baraga established a Catholic Mission, and for decades it was simply known as the Catholic Mission. Baraga lived in the mission for a short time, and it was there that he wrote an Ojibwe dictionary that was published in 1853. The dictionary remains an important tool for translating the Ojibwe and Chippewa language into English to this day. In 1894, the mission was given a post office and officially named Assinins after the Indian Chief.

The village started with several log cabins and a church. In 1860, Baraga built the St. Joseph Orphanage and School. The original building was destroyed by fire, and a new larger stone building was built to replace it along with a rectory and convent. In 1929, another large three story orphanage was built and at its peak had 950 orphans, both Native American and white children. The structures were last used in the 1960s and in recent years have collapsed. Only a small portion of the orphanage is still standing hidden behind the trees. The area is now part of the Keweenaw Bay Indian Community and is listed as a National Historic District.

Central Mine

Location:
US-41 and Central Road About five
miles north of Phoenix
47.405692, -88.2003367

US-41 is the main road through the center of the
Keweenaw Peninsula. Travelers along the road may notice
a little sign for the Central Mine Visitors Center located
between Calumet and Copper Harbor. Many tourists pass

by without even thinking of stopping. I think few people realize there is a whole ghost town to explore that is open to the public.

In 1854, John Shawson, a local miner, discovered copper in the region, and the Central Mining Company was formed. A company town was built around the mining operation and given the same name as the company. The town's population grew to over nine hundred people. More than one hundred structures were built, which included houses, mining buildings and a church. Many of the miners were immigrants from Cornwall, England, bringing with them their pasty recipes. The meat filled pastry is popular in the Upper Peninsula. By the late 1890s, the copper had been depleted, and Central Mine turned off the pumps and sealed the shafts. By 1950, the last permanent residents had left the once prosperous town.

The Keweenaw County Historical Society owns thirty-eight acres of the old Central Mine site and town. It operates the Visitors Center which is located in a former house. The society has also restored several other houses and buildings in the old town. Some are open to visitors and decorated with antiques from the period they were built. When I visited, the small town was strangely quiet. I could walk through the open houses and explore the area. It was like stepping back in time. Visitors can walk into a house over a century old and see items on display that date back to the mining days.

If you visit be sure to stop by the Visitors Center first and look at the map since some of the property is private and closed to tourists.

Historic Fayette

Location:
Fayette State Park
4785 II Road (M-183)
Garden, MI 49835
45.717657, -86.667932

The largest ghost town in Michigan is Fayette in the Garden Peninsula, which juts out into Lake Michigan along the southern part of the Upper Peninsula. Fayette is about twenty miles south of US-2 and was started by the

Jackson Iron Company in 1867. After the Civil War, iron and steel were in high demand. The site, located in Snail Shell Harbor, was an ideal spot for an iron furnace and shipping harbor. The town was named after Fayette Brown, one of the company's directors.

In the late 1800s, the town grew to have over five hundred residents, most of whom worked for the Jackson Iron Company. Workers smelted the iron ore in the town's furnace to produce pig iron, which was used to make steel. Pig iron was more efficient to ship than raw iron ore. The name pig iron comes from the shapes of the ingots in which the iron was poured. They looked like little piglets, so the name stuck.

The town continued producing pig iron until the early 1890s. By that time, much of the timber used to fire the furnaces had been harvested. In addition to the dwindling firewood supply, more efficient methods of producing iron and steel had been created, and the town of Fayette was no longer profitable. Without any work, most of the residents moved away, and Fayette became more of a summer resort as people began enjoying the natural beauty surrounding the former iron smelting community. By the 1950s, the town had been purchased by the Escanaba Paper Company, which gave it to the Michigan government in exchange for timberland.

The historic town of Fayette is now part of Fayette State Park. It includes twenty buildings, of which nineteen are original. The buildings are open for visitors to tour and see what life was like in the early 1900s iron smelting town.

Payment Settlement

Location:
Holy Angels Church
10164 E. Northshore Drive
Sault Ste. Marie, MI 49783
46.5273689, -84.1511357

Sugar Island sits east of Sault Ste. Marie on the other side of the St Marys River. It is one of the largest islands along the river that shares a border with Canada. The island is about six miles wide and thirteen miles long.

In 1845, Michael Payment moved to Sugar Island and established a small settlement on the northern tip of the island known at the time as "Payment's Landing" or "Payment Settlement." Bishop Baraga was a frequent visitor to the settlement. In 1856, after purchasing lumber, he asked Payment to construct a little wooden church. The church was used continuously until 1953, when it was closed. It was reopened in 1982 and used for annual Masses to celebrate Bishop Baraga's birthday. The church is currently called Holy Angels Roman Catholic Church, but it was originally called Church of Our Savior, Friend of Children. It still stands at the northern tip of the island. A trail behind the church leads to an old cemetery where some of the island's early inhabitants are laid to rest.

The Sugar Islander II car ferry transports vehicles across the St. Mary's River to Sugar Island. For $20 you can ride the ferry, in your car, over to the island and back. The island was named Sisibakmatominis (maple sugar island translated into English) by the Chippewas for its abundant maple trees.

Nonesuch

Location:
Porcupine Mountains
Wilderness State Park
Parking area off South
Boundary Rd.
46.7582592, -89.6196294

The Porcupine Mountains in the western Upper Peninsula is the largest state park in Michigan. It's known for hiking trails, waterfalls, and the Lake Of The Clouds. Few people know that hidden among the trees are the ruins of an old mining town. The town of Nonesuch was created when mining near the Little Iron River began in 1867. The town and mine were named for nonesuch, a type of copper ore that exists in sandstone.

At its peak, the town had a population of 300 people. Along with the mining buildings, the small town had a school, boarding houses, stables, and even a baseball team. Extracting the fine copper particles out of the sandstone was a labor intensive process, and by 1912, the mine had closed.

Stone walls and cast iron machine parts from the mine can still be found in the area where the town once stood. The best way to get to the ruins is to take South Boundary

Nonesuch mill circa 1900 Photo from the National Park Service

Road east from the visitors center. Where the road curves south, you will find a dirt road that leads to a parking area with some signage for the old mine. A footpath about a half-mile long leads to the historic mine site.

Watson and Woodlawn

Old buildings in the town of Watson

Location:
Watson
Intersection of County Road 426 and SI near Cornell Michigan
46.019302, -87.414477

Woodlawn
Intersection of County Road 426 and Cedardale 28th Rd near Cornell Michigan
45.94208807, -87.2969451

Watson is nestled in the south-east corner of Marquette County on Road 426. It has an old general store that looks like it closed a few decades ago. An abandoned house and a couple of empty buildings still remain standing in the long forgotten community. A "mail distribution point" was located in the Watson Store Company prior to 1918. I wonder if that is the decaying store that is still standing.

A handful of people still live in the area, and the Watson Bible Chapel is nearby. A set of railroad tracks run next to Road 426, but with the grass and trees growing up between the rails, the train has not traveled down them in a long time. I am assuming after the train no longer stopped in Watson, the people in the little town slowly moved away. It is a reminder of days gone by, and I hope it continues to stand for many years.

Southeast of Watson on County Road 426 is an old two story building with a green roof. It stands in the trees on the other side of the railroad tracks. At one time it was the Escanaba & Lake Superior Railroad, but it looks as if it has been a long time since a train traveled down them. I

Old house near the former town of Woodlawn

found an old county map that shows the name of the town of Woodlawn. The town was originally called White, but the name was changed to Woodlawn when it got a post office in 1905. I am wondering if the old building was a boarding house, but it looks as if it has been a long time since anyone slept overnight in it.

The trip from Cornell to Channing along County Road 426 passes through many old towns, or at least they were towns at one time. If you love exploring back roads, then this is a road in the Upper Peninsula you need to drive down.

Winona

Location:
Winona Road Elm River
Township

Old Building ruins
46.87619099, -88.9043429

The town of Winona sits at the base of the Keweenaw
Peninsula near Twin Lakes. There are a few houses and
about thirteen residents, but for the most part, it is a
ghost town. During its heyday in the 1920s, it had about a
thousand residents and restaurants, a brewery, sports

teams, churches, boarding houses, a train depot, a saloon, stores, boardwalks, a school, and a barber shop. The town of Winona sprung up around the mines that were started in 1864. The mine closed in 1923, and soon after the town began to dwindle, and eventually almost everyone moved away. I saw this old building being consumed by the forest on D Street. I am not sure what it was, but it's rather large, so maybe a store or boarding house. In the woods hidden by the trees are foundations of some of the buildings of the forgotten mining town.

Herman

The old store near the railroad tracks

Location:
17448 Lystila
L'Anse, MI 49946
46.66668779, -88.36675142

Herman is located in a remote section of the Huron Mountains between L'Anse and Nestoria. The town was named for Finnish lumberjack Herman Keranen, who purchased forty acres and began farming in the area. The Duluth, South Shore and Atlantic Railroad Company ran tracks past the town and was the primary way of getting in and out. The town got a post office in 1904 and built a school. The Herman Athletic Association was organized in 1912 and a farmer's cooperative association in 1919. Herman Hall is a historical building constructed in 1931

Herman circa 1940, Old store in the center and the Dantes house on the right

The Dantes House

by members of a Finnish Amateur Athletic Society. The hall has been recognized by historians in Finland and in the U.S. as one of the best surviving "Finn Halls" in the country. The hall still stands in the town today, and it hosts the annual Hunters Stew Feast in November.

Over the decades, the population has dwindled, and it is mostly a ghost town. A few people continue to live in the historic community. The old store still stands by the railroad tracks, although it closed years ago. The train still passes through but no longer stops in Herman.

A large old house sits in the town of Herman. This is the old Dantes house and it is named for its original resident,

Charles T Dantes, who was a Finn from Northern Sweden who settled in Herman in 1907. He worked for the railroad and owned the general store. He was the town's postmaster, and sheriff of Baraga County.

Herman is located off Nestoria Herman Road. It angles through the Huron Mountains and looks like a shortcut to L'Anse. US-41 heads west and then turns north to L'Anse. While Nestoria Herman Road looks faster on a map, it is a winding, hilly dirt road through the forest. It is definitely not faster, but it is a fun drive if you like to go exploring. I recommend having a four wheel drive truck or SUV if you take it.

On December 19, 1996, the town received one of the largest snowfalls in Michigan history, with 30 inches of the white stuff falling in the single day.

Stalwart

Location:
Stalwart Cemetery
8457 M-48,
Goetzville, MI 49736
46.0933524, -84.2387934

An old building that was a store at one time stands on M-48 between Pickford and Goetzville in the eastern side of the Upper Peninsula. It is a reminder of the old town of Stalwart and the hearty families that homesteaded the area. In 1878, Richard Hanna, John Johnston, William

147

Scott and John Scott were the first men to trek into the swampy wilderness to homestead the area. The following year, more families began homesteading, but it was not an easy task to get to their land. At the time, no roads existed through the rugged terrain. They used horses and oxen pulling jumpers to transport their belongings. Jumpers were large wooden sleds that could be dragged over the ground. Thomas Forgrave and John McKenzie carried a cookstove on two poles for about five miles to their new home.

In 1881, Edgar J. Swart, postmaster at Prentis Bay at the time, and John J. McKenzie made an application for a post office for the new settlement. They applied for the name Garfield in honor of President James A. Garfield, but it was denied because there was already a town with that name. They next tried the name Arthur for President Chester A. Arthur, but that too had been taken. The Post Office Department at Washington, D.C. responded back to the settlers with the name of Stalwart, because president Arthur was in the Stalwart factor of the Republican party, and it would still be named for him.

In 1898, a school was built on the Tripp family farm. The children had both the summers and the winters off. School started in September and ended in the latter part of November. It started back up around the 15th of April and ended in June. I imagine it would have been difficult to walk to school in the middle of winter in the U.P.

Over time, it was easier to drive to and from Stalwart in modern cars on paved roads. Many of the local businesses closed and the children went to school in other cities. Some of the descendants of the original settlers still live in the area, and the old store and cemetery stand as a reminder of the early days of Stalwart.

The town still holds the annual agricultural fair every september. They have been hosting it since 1905.

Emerson

Emerson circa 1880

Location:
Historical Marker near M-123
about a half mile south of
where it crosses the
Tahquamenon River
46.5534836, -85.0346241

Next to M-123 about a half mile south of where it crosses the Tahquamenon River is a historical marker for the town of Emerson. It was founded by Kurt Emerson, a lumberman from the Saginaw Bay area in the 1880s. He built a sawmill and in 1884 sold his establishment to the

Chesbrough Lumber Company. The town prospered cutting the logs that were floated down the Tahquamenon River. By 1890, the town had a population of 250 and had a post office, general store and school. There were no roads to the town so they had to get supplies by ships sailing in and out of town when Lake Superior was not frozen.

By 1912, the timber had all been cut, and the mill closed in 1912. Although many residents moved away, the town had a second life as a fishing village. The post office closed in 1914, and a new school was built in Paradise in 1927 where the children of Emerson now attended. By 1947, only 25 people lived in Emerson, and the land surrounding it was deeded to the state and became part of

Chesbrough Lumber Company in Emerson circa 1880

Tahquamenon Falls State Park. By the 1950s, the town was completely abandoned and the remaining buildings were moved or demolished.

The only thing that remains are the foundations of a building on a small island offshore south of the mouth of the Tahquamenon River. I have seen references claim that it is the foundation of a sawmill, but it makes more sense that it was part of a fishery. Whatever it was, it sits as a silent reminder of the once busy town.

A trail leads to the shore from the historical marker to where the town once stood. Unfortunately, it is usually wet and muddy and difficult to hike most of the summer.

Old Victoria

Location:
25401 Victoria Dam Rd,
Victoria, MI 49960
46.703097, -89.2281115

About four miles southwest of Rockland near the Ontonagon River is the historic Old Victoria townsite. It was the site of one of Michigan's first copper mines when Englishman Alexander Henry discovered the "Ontonagon Boulder" nearby in 1766, an enormous boulder of pure copper known to the Indians as "Manitoti". In 1843, the

Ontonagon Boulder was transported by the U.S. government to the Smithsonian in Washington D.C. A few companies attempted to mine the area in the 1850s. By 1899, they had consolidated into the Victoria Mining Company, and a town was built to support the mine and its workers.

Named after the mining company, Victoria grew to over eighty homes, a school, church and a general store. The mine produced copper for several years, and the town prospered. After World War I, the mine was shut down because it was no longer profitable. By 1921, the town was abandoned and the home and buildings left to the demise of Mother Nature. In 1965, a group of local residents began restoring the townsite, and it is now open to the public as a museum. The town offers a unique glimpse into the history of copper mining in the region. It is open daily from June to October.

Conclusion

Visiting these historic and forgotten places makes me wonder about the people who lived at them. It must have been a hard life in Michigan before modern electricity, roads and indoor plumbing. Seeing some of the old buildings and schools in remote locations reminds me that the people who came before us had to survive harsh and difficult conditions. Heading out on a road trip and traveling through some of Michigan's small villages and ghost towns is a great way to learn about Michgian's past.

I am still exploring the Great Lakes State and searching places I have not visited. There are a lot of wonderful and interesting things to see. Michigan is a large state from Detroit to the Keweenaw in the Upper Peninsula, and there are still a lot of roads I have not driven down. I hope you will continue to follow my journey at www.lostinmichigan.net.

I have also been exploring other states, and you can follow my journey through them at www.lostinthestates.com.

Continue following
my journey at

www.lostinmichigan.net

To follow my travels outside of
Michigan you can visit

www.lostinthestates.com